ELVIS PRESLEY™

T0065906

ISBN 978-1-4950-7685-5

7777 W. BLUEMOUND RD. P.O. BOX 13819 MILWAUKEE, WI 53213

Visit Hal Leonard Online at
www.halleonard.com

BLUE SUEDE SHOES

Words and Music by
CARL LEE PERKINS

mp *Solo ends*

cresc.

mf

CAN'T HELP FALLING IN LOVE
from the Paramount Picture BLUE HAWAII

Words and Music by GEORGE DAVID WEISS,
HUGO PERETTI and LUIGI CREATORE

CRYIN' IN THE CHAPEL

Words and Music by
ARTIE GLENN

DON'T

Words and Music by JERRY LEIBER
and MIKE STOLLER

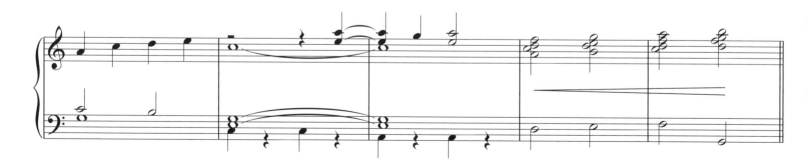

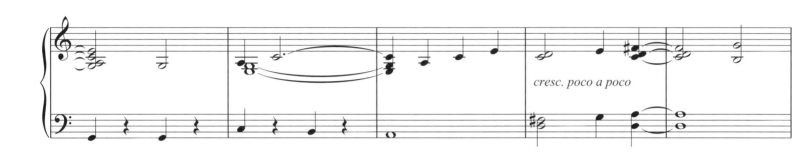

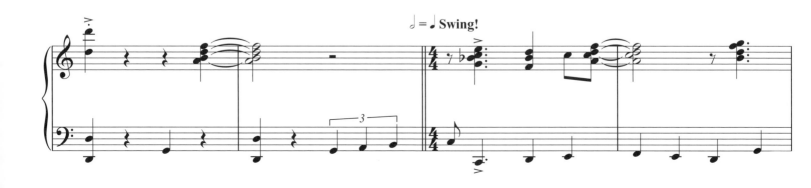

Tempo I (♩ = ♪)

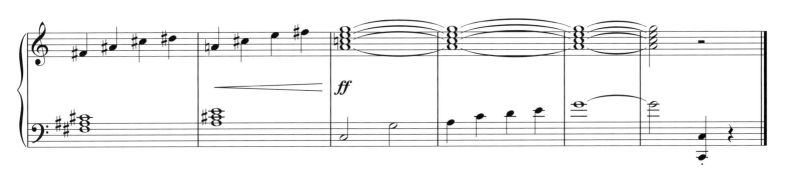

DON'T BE CRUEL
(To a Heart That's True)

Words and Music by OTIS BLACKWELL
and ELVIS PRESLEY

Solo ad lib.

mf

f

Solo ends

HEARTBREAK HOTEL

Words and Music by MAE BOREN AXTON,
TOMMY DURDEN and ELVIS PRESLEY

Salsa (♩ = 92)

Pedal only as needed

SUSPICIOUS MINDS

Words and Music by
FRANCIS ZAMBON

Moderate Blues Shuffle (♩ = 108)

Pedal only as needed

I WANT YOU, I NEED YOU, I LOVE YOU

Words and Music by MAURICE MYSELS
and IRA KOSLOFF

JAILHOUSE ROCK

Words and Music by JERRY LEIBER
and MIKE STOLLER

Solo ad lib.

8va- -

(8va)- -

p sub.

Solo ends

mp

LOVE ME TENDER

Words and Music by ELVIS PRESLEY
and VERA MATSON

THE WONDER OF YOU

Words and Music by
BAKER KNIGHT

YOU DON'T HAVE TO SAY YOU LOVE ME

English Words by VICKI WICKHAM and SIMON NAPIER-BELL
Original Italian Words by V. PALLAVICINI
Music by P. DONAGGIO

Slowly and freely

Slow Swing (♩ = 72)

Double-time feel, Swing 16ths

ALL JAZZED UP!

FROM HAL LEONARD

In this series, pop hits receive unexpected fresh treatments. Uniquely reimagined and crafted for intermediate piano solo, these favorites have been All Jazzed Up!

J.S. BACH
Air on the G String • Aria • Bist du bei mir (Be Thou with Me) • Gavotte • Jesu, Joy of Man's Desiring • Largo • March • Minuet in G • Musette • Sheep May Safely Graze • Siciliano • Sleepers, Awake (Wachet Auf).
00151064..$12.99

THE BEATLES
All My Loving • And I Love Her • Come Together • Eight Days a Week • Eleanor Rigby • The Fool on the Hill • Here, There and Everywhere • Lady Madonna • Lucy in the Sky with Diamonds • Michelle • While My Guitar Gently Weeps • Yesterday.
00172235..$12.99

COLDPLAY
Clocks • Don't Panic • Every Teardrop Is a Waterfall • Fix You • Magic • Paradise • The Scientist • A Sky Full of Stars • Speed of Sound • Trouble • Viva La Vida • Yellow.
00149026..$12.99

DISNEY
Belle • Circle of Life • Cruella De Vil • Ev'rybody Wants to Be a Cat • It's a Small World • Let It Go • Mickey Mouse March • Once upon a Dream • Part of Your World • Supercalifragilisticexpialidocious • Under the Sea • When She Loved Me.
00151072..$12.99

JIMI HENDRIX
Castles Made of Sand • Crosstown Traffic • Fire • Foxey Lady • Hey Joe • Little Wing • Manic Depression • Purple Haze • Spanish Castle Magic • The Wind Cries Mary.
00174441..$12.99

BILLY JOEL
And So It Goes • Honesty • It's Still Rock and Roll to Me • Just the Way You Are • The Longest Time • Lullabye (Goodnight, My Angel) • My Life • New York State of Mind • Piano Man • The River of Dreams • She's Always a Woman • She's Got a Way.
00149039..$12.99

MOTOWN
Ain't Nothing like the Real Thing • How Sweet It Is (To Be Loved by You) • I Can't Help Myself (Sugar Pie, Honey Bunch) • I Heard It Through the Grapevine • I Want You Back • Let's Get It On • My Girl • Never Can Say Goodbye • Overjoyed • Papa Was a Rollin' Stone • Still • You Can't Hurry Love.
00174482..$12.99

NIRVANA
About a Girl • All Apologies • Come as You Are • Dumb • Heart Shaped Box • In Bloom • Lithium • The Man Who Sold the World • On a Plain • (New Wave) Polly • Rape Me • Smells like Teen Spirit.
00149025..$12.99

OZZY OSBOURNE
Crazy Train • Dreamer • Flying High Again • Goodbye to Romance • Iron Man • Mama, I'm Coming Home • Mr. Crowley • No More Tears • Over the Mountain • Paranoid • Perry Mason • Time After Time.
00149040..$12.99

STEVIE WONDER
As • Ebony and Ivory • For Once in My Life • I Just Called to Say I Love You • I Wish • Isn't She Lovely • My Cherie Amour • Ribbon in the Sky • Signed, Sealed, Delivered I'm Yours • Sir Duke • Superstition • You Are the Sunshine of My Life.
00149090..$12.99

www.halleonard.com

Prices, contents and availability subject to change without notice.

Disney characters and artwork © Disney Enterprises, Inc.